Overheard in a Drugstore

Also by Andrew Glaze

Andrew Glaze: Greatest Hits 1964–2004 (2005)

Remembering Thunder (2002)

Someone Will Go On Owing: Selected Poems, 1966–1992 (1998)

Reality Street (1991)

Earth That Sings: On the Poetry of Andrew Glaze (1985)

A City (1982)

I Am the Jefferson County Courthouse and Other Poems (1981)

The Trash Dragon of Shensi (1978)

A Masque of Surgery: Poems and Translations (1974)

Damned Ugly Children (1966)

Lines/Poems:
Poems by Andrew Glaze & Engravings by Umaña (1964)

The Token, a Selection of Verse (1963)

OVERHEARD IN A DRUGSTORE

And Other Poems

ANDREW GLAZE

NewSouth Books

Montgomery

NewSouth Books
105 S. Court Street
Montgomery, AL 36104

Acknowledgments:
Some of the poems in this volume were originally published in the following:
Andrew Glaze: Greatest Hits 1964–2004, "Alleluia"; *Big City Lit,* "Fishermen,"
"Bears"; *Birmingham Arts Journal,* "Issa," "Hard Times," "Trap of Feathers";
Birmingham Poetry Review, "Trees"; *Birmingham Weekly,* "You're Never With
Who You Want to Be"; *Boston /96,* "Garcia" (re-titled Garcia's Store"); *HYN
Anthology & New York Muse* "Tomorrow I'll Be Gone"; *Light,* "You're Never with
Who You Want to Be"; *New York Quarterly,* "Witches," "Nursing Home" (retitled
"The Banderlog"), "Groucho"; *Negative Capability,* "If Suffering Is to Love";
Pivot, "The View From Straw's," "Epic," "Seamstress" (retitled "Seamstress of
Shine"); *Poetry Magazine,* "Antigua" (re-titled "A Visit to Barbados"); *Spirituality
& Health,* "Alleluia"; *Sulfur City Review,* "Piñata," "Goddam Pretty," "Blue
Ridge,"; *Trails & Timberline Quarterly,* "A Place That Can't Be Bought" (retitled
"Rudderless"); *TriQuarterly76,* "Nursing Home" (retitled "The Banderlog");
Turtlehouse Press, "Overheard in a Drugstore," "Mr. Frost."

Publisher's Cataloging-in-Publication data

Glaze, Andrew
Overheard in a drugstore : and other poems / Andew Glaze.
p. cm.

ISBN 978-1-60306-399-9 (paperback)
ISBN 978-1-60306-400-2 (ebook)

1. Poetry. I. Title.

2015946966

Edited by Elizabeth Glaze

Design by Randall Williams

Printed in the United States of America
by Bang Printing

To my children, Betsy and Peter,

and their children and spouses Charles and Kate,

and to Arlen and Bill with thanks.

Contents

I

FACULTY AND FELLOWS, 1946 BREAD LOAF WRITERS' CONFERENCE
Rear: Robert Frost, Robert Bordner, Graeme Lorimer, Andrew Glaze, Wallace Stegner, Rudolph Kieve, Theodore Morrison, Eugene Burdick, William Sloane. Front: Carol Warren Burdick, Kay Morrison, Helen Everitt, Mary Stegner. (Used by permission of Middlebury College Special Collections and Archives)

While at Harvard, Andrew Glaze met Robert Frost through a series of poetry student dinners and again at the 1946 Bread Loaf Writer's Conference. In the mid-1950s, on a poetry tour, Frost had his Birmingham host contact Glaze to invite him on an excursion to Jasper, Alabama. In 2010, Glaze learned of the existence of Frost's 1956 note (opposite), which had been donated to Dartmouth by the wife of Glaze's Harvard poetry teacher, Theodore Morrison. One must assume it was part of a private exchange between Morrison and Robert Frost discussing poems that made their way into Glaze's first published book.

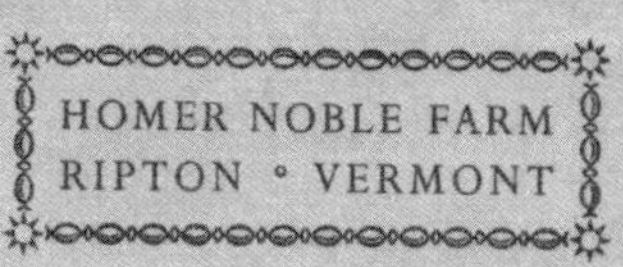

"*I should be sorry if a book of verse as genuine and readable as this couldn't find a publisher. I have high hopes of Mr. Glaze. Robert Frost, April 14, 1956.*" *(By permission of the Robert Frost Estate; photo courtesy of the Rauner Library at Dartmouth)*

Mr. Frost

An undocumented biographical note

Mister Frost, like most champions of the prize,
was a large person, towering over the miniscule
poets skittering about the local minstrelsy.
One day, a gaggle of them,
worked out a magisterial moment for him to meet
an ancient rebel confederate; it was said,
alive on this earth a hundred and seven years.
They wished to scrabble up the usual TV detritus
about a New England bard discussing
the unlikelihood that there was a still extant
rebel miner, out in the dumps and pea patches
of the Appalachian crags. —But when they got there,
they found it was only an old black man
of a hundred and seven years who lived in a wooden
piano box on half an acre of ravine
covered in pine slash, out Jasper way.
He raised a dozen chickens, had a hacking cough,
and the two of them got talking what it meant to be old.
"You've got to keep moving," said Mr. Frost.
"Else your bones will freeze," agreed the old man.
"How do you eat?" said Mr. Frost.
"Oh, that ain't so hard," the centenarian replied.
"I use my welfare to buy me chicken feed,
and I has an egg for breakfast, lunch and dinner.
It wouldn't be so bad if it wasn't for my lungs,
they awfully full of itchy dust from the mines.
It seems like nothing but whisky will cut the dust."

Mr. Frost ruminated a moment,
then held up his hand as if someone
had started to speak. "The principle is," he said,
"that I think we should leave this gentleman alone.
He's got his life pretty well licked into shape,
and as a pledge of concern and farewell,
I'll buy him a bottle of whisky," said Mr. Frost.

Love

Sometime, along the way,
though love poems may flap and squawk, then escape,
along in years, with luck,
the ghost of one, somehow may come skittering back.
Liquid as mist, its phantom will rise,
the stinks you've remembered as bitter
will be dried and perfumed like wild grass.

Long-forgotten names and places
will ache to come spilling out
and the hosts of oblivion once more will speak.
Old songs will mutter themselves into life
remembering dreams, and when that time awakens,
you'll come to swear to yourself

that something has shifted weight
at the earth's center.
While the harmony lasts,
what you dream you will seem to touch,
what evanesces will seem to endure forever.

Though it takes life for only a moment or so,
as it awakes from its wraithy home
you'll once more shudder and sing,
and out of its ghostly enchanted world,
remember the miracle of speech.

BLUE RIDGE

— a lament.

It's the best road between truckways climbing into miles,
and here come Buckthorn, Hemlock, Mountain Laurel,
    Rhododendron,
shotgunning everywhere, into light and dark,
our motor's let-up punctuated with Red-eyed Vireos,
Summer Tanagers, Warblers, the occasional ghost of a Raven.

Far below, tractors grumble, pickups scurry,
and blue smoke rises from verandahed motels,
hot instant chicken, bible colleges, refineries,
and suburbs. At the other verge,
eerily coming off the blind side uphill, flow boundless forests,
and endless divisions of blue-gray butternut armies.

Racketing with fierce crashes of musketry,
they clatter behind risings, dashing across
bare hills in patterns of horses.
Tiny caissons crawl, shuddering past,
bent with piles of the bloody wounded and dead,
creaking to the bullet-shattered gossamer whinings of fife.

It's a vision of the kingdom we come from,
the republic we have been setting out for.
Two ghostly realms divided
by a mystic ridge, running along between
two terrible fates, like a double brink.

What does it want from us? Pointless to weep,
pointless to blame. The vision clears, rises
like wood smoke, and does not disband.
And still it's there, awaiting, as we enter the machine again,
and move off through leaf-doors and walls of shadow play.

Climbing the Sky

for Irene Latham

Leaving from Cauterets, up to the South,
after the first traverse
we left the takers of the waters
like trader ants below.
Ascending the causeway,
dangling cups like aluminum chains,
up the crystal skies
we passed the toffee-folding machines,
up through the bushy slopes
leaving below the running waiters and steaming
chicory blenders retreating behind us and beneath.

Up the thunder-reverberating bowl of the pic de luz,
the whole world behind was shrinking,
like a cupboard tucked in a fringe of grass,
then bent beneath and fell away,
and we were in another world of long green slopes,
world-weary yellow fields that fibrillated
in the smoke of the August tingling air.

Far away to north, the blunt hills were reduced by space
into rhythmic demi-bubbles of France.
The sun buzzed from the South,
great too, in its own right,

and north and south the feral sisters tramped away
one next to another like great
brown bears of the Pyrenees.
We walked the tightrope of a col, and there we were,
arrived at last—in the pockets of vastness
anchored to the earth only by air.

Joyous

Overhead the sun bursts its bonds,
a cloud buries its foolish face in nothing,
and something hurries off to connive at day.

Life's ugly beggar hurries his way around the block,
playing a vast charade,
the only one that matters.

Day, in its ridiculous vastness,
swears it is finished, done,
though it's more alive than anything we do.

And that, this world swears, is correct, neat, and sensible.
Taste and carry it with you,
for it's the heart of the universe,
the happiness of every blessed lie we warrant to be true.

Looking for Fire

We'd lost our fire
and so must journey for more,
from far off.
On the second day
there came a monstrous creaking
through the barren gulleys,
which as we got nearer to it for many leagues
grew into a vast booming.

Then at last, from behind the top
of a fold in the mountain
we peered across a wide swale
to where there stood an enormous man
in the valley underneath.
His skin was like battered hardwood,
where should have been brows
were only bald, scarred hummocks—
where should have been eyes
were dusky caves
pushed inward with blind rage.

He kept endlessly forcing around and around
a great wheel made of wood,
of tree trunks like hill-roots.
Gripping it by the knobs of its burls,
he forced the thing forward and down
so the formless block
shuddering with frictions,
turned as in an ungreased hole,

gusting a column of blue,
interrupted by smoke.
Still, no flame, no fire!

It was as with us!
His shoulders streamed with pebbles of sweat,
his brute muscles teemed, coiled and writhed,
his wild face shook with anguish,
and baffled rage.
Far down in the earth
echoed a bellowing and groaning.

We were afraid,
but coming to the far dike, beholding his suffering,
which we could not help,
all of us, joining him from afar,
as though we understood,
—broke into tears.

Hope is a catch in the trap of feathers.
The mockingbird keeps wandering song to song
Beneath the stinging forgetfulness of the moon.
An owl goes passing, quivering soft wings and a "chunk."

What name to give the unexplainable rapture,
Making the skin crawl with its amalgam of death and failure
Fluttering in the pulse.
Soon enough we're trapped in our own running,
By what we call happiness,
The girdling hedge of desperation.

Something is trying to make its way
From where we are to where we're going to be.
Is it real? What is it and where is it bound,
That so splendidly awakens
Reaching behind and ahead of us
Off into the hinterlands of night?

Waltz of the Sensible

Once, holding Reason's ugly hand and skipping,
I went wind-hassled down wet sidewalks,
trying to keep it out of sailor's bars, by force.

It called me a wimp,
laid back the sheets to point
to the skeleton waiting there,
showed how that old death bone
gnashed its chops
ready to be embraced.

Said ambition, happiness, hope, and singing,
all of them, each in turn, was a lie,
held out Eternity's hand like a Pope
and promised the lollipop kingdom!

But only a part of me was reason's child.
All the rest kept shouting "Damn you, thief,
—I'd rather be singing shouting, ranting hellos,
than ever lie down with some such scurrilous bedfellow
whose only hello was memories of goodbye."

Manhattan above Manhattan—a Triptych

1) Up From Sandy Hook

There is a Manhattan above Manhattan,
it towers over my imagination.
Smoke trails away from its tiny towers,
like double twin-stacked snails of power.
They are come, arriving,
—arrival not being intended, —
beggared by a regretful sting.

Across two bays there stands a bronze lady
brandishing a torch. She's full of stairways,
people slithering about her vitalities and privacies.
Arch priestess of plumbing;
Bartholdi's comically extravagant
wizardess of emerald sheen.
Oh, Monster of torch and book,
Dear Lady, we've arrived, not wanting it particularly,
but nailing the tattered banner to the masthead,
for someone coming along but not yet about to be.

Its Manhattan towers over my Manhattan
like a mirror. Reeling like a sloop,
I roll over, rise, and scramble—each scuffed knee every minute,
        becoming less ocean,
and more of American earth.
Some of the molecules that make me
are set to become parts of clouds about heights

to wash up on beaches I never saw.
I shall slide down into the multiple oceans.
Distance will disclose how it rises up there.

2) Grant's Angel

The coppery sun above the palisades and Nyack
uplifts the waters of Tappan Zee, and out
from the gray-green smoking waste of rock
tells Washington Heights the time of day.
The fire spells out the time of the year,
and like a solemn doctor above in the day,
the altitudes huddle and mutter,
marking their almanacs with the strict red weather.

Somewhere east of Grant's Tomb
on a coppery roof, one trumpeting angel squats,
seated upon the ultimate ridge,
and grapples between his hams the sharp knife of the roof.
With anxious coppery cheek, he waits for the haze to lift.
He's not given up expecting, and lifts his eyes
up past the latticed belfry, conning the slate blue air
for the least sign of penitence.

There's a rigid, blank-faced choir of Byzantine acolytes
in the western door of the tabernacle across the street,
but he looks above their stare
with motionless disapproving eyes.
He thinks they are dying of that fixed smile, —
what for, those endless beatitudes? Like any honest angel,
he prefers to seek nearby the site where the sun's fire

is streaming down rock, rail, and spire,
dispensing absolution across the kingdoms of air.

3) Battery Park

The band, played out like sleepy arguments,
now splits in pieces as it frazzles away,
the sun boiling down to a sulfurous pit of orange,
idles a chuffing of brimstone smoke,
and the waiting darkness wraps itself
about the blackened fringes like a shawl.
Of a sudden, somewhere far off, there's an anvil thump,
noisily falling in the smith's fire pit,

and flicking and whizzing, a bonfire rose contentedly blooms,
—pops, flinging zillions of starry dimes.
A squirrel of fire scurries up the pall,
printing tiny footprints across the cinder,

and the sky bellows again with thundering cuffs,
blue pom-poms and pink sleek silks opening like umbrellas.
Dandelion blossoms sizzle across a purple mead,
sullenly burning, at which once again, the darkness yawns,

and curls itself across the zenith like a sleeping child,
leaving only a rumor of danger and control.
Atop it all, fiercely rattles across, a helicopter.
It bands athwart the fragrant ebony night,
and like an electric wasp, stings the moon.

II

ALLELUIA

As I walk mornings down Bleecker Street,
I meet ten saints with filthy demands.
The tenements shout with holiness,
God reels by or sleeps on the curb,
at home everywhere in the wrecks and bars,
in the stale tobacco and business,
and everything that's wild and absurd,
like madness with madness and holding hands.

I had rather ten faces than ten birds,
I don't sense deliverance in a tree.
There is no impossible in lakes,
there is more miracle in a crowd
than in a Rocky Mountain or me.
There is more holiness in an eye
than in a scroll of holy words.
God's here, thank God, in the market place!
Viva the Signor of warts and turds!

Garcia's Store

Garcia the storekeeper,
below my window every day at the curb
sweeping before the sun gets up,
patiently gathers bottles,
the broken shiver-stars
of yesterday's do-nothings,
who sleep as ever, across the hoods
of parked cars.
His wife, getting up late, with gummy eyes,
stands in the doorway trading the time of day
with customers, children, loafers, and dogs.
Garcia's indolent son, a sort of tire-man of waist fat,
will squat upon his black motorbike.
It's his third this year. His Fu Manchu mustache
and unshaved dirty cheeks will squeeze out
from under the helmet,
shading a cloud of greasy black hair.

Every day, Garcia watches it all serenely,
his hollow cheeks are withered.
He sells coconut bars and chicken wings,
peers through his dirty glasses
across sales slip figures, with his
naked gums and two teeth.
Twice this year they've come in under the floor,

and skipped away with a dozen cases of his beer.
He shrugs, sniffs, and nails up a network of two-by-fours.

At nine in the night, he stands by the adding machine
figuring the day, talking to Anselmo
the numbers runner, who leans over his cane,
rubbing his white fuzz of hair.
Garcia fumbles the numbers into the machine,
takes out the paper,
peers at it under his glasses,
licks his lips, says OK, shakes his head
with a sort of benediction.
Then he puts on his red woodsman's jacket,
slams the gate and sets the burglar alarm.
Never does it go off with a moonlight celebration
of a burglar. It rings by itself
many a night at 4 a.m.
Garcia will patiently rise up out of his bed
and float like a wraith around the corner to set it again.
When he leaves, he will hesitate,
then pat his door gently,
like quieting a restless, sleepless child.

Listen!

The sun boils down,
and up straddles the moon,
like an ice lump
floating across the hungry wood.
A mockingbird's crooked roulade
putters across the white, gleaming,
its lonely serenades
making the skin quicken.

Suddenly,
with no warning—
God—stately—has stopped his dancing,
undoes for an instant the owl's rape,
the wolf's rasp, the day's delusion.
At the abyss our stubborn hearts waver,
we salute in his honor
whatever wakens and sleeps.

Epic

The rooftop starlings swirl up and shiver,
trying to understand with stammering wings,
and the clouds are writing themselves into speech
across a sky like a stone-cold slate.

Suddenly from someplace beyond reach,
a sort of singing, a sort of revelation,
as though somewhere a door opens or shuts
or drifts away, and when I attempt to see,
nothing's changed in the least.

Yet behind my back in the dark sky without a trace
no matter how quickly I turn, —
(vanishing when I look at the dark empty sky),
a thousand wild and stately sunsets
are taking place.

Days of Being Born

The first day of being born is sun,
falling out over garden ash and trees,
bidding farewell to snowdrift,
hiring representations out of the wind.

Advancing into the world with no expectation,
its first walk is random,
un-glittering, not well-advised,
and next it learns spinning, like a Catherine wheel.

It calculates tricks, and subtly spills out its pockets,
of scatter-shots loans.
Its earliest welcome comes streaming,
beginning with only a whisper,
already it's risen to a well-sprung humming.

And then all at once, as though learning to brood,
it awakens.
Loosed in the enormous, nesting sky,
it rustles a tall order of birds and wings.

Hard Times

I thank fortune for hard times,
luck for breaking my granite pride,
fear for making me strong, long enough
to be absurd, careless, and when I think of it—kind.

Also, bless you, goodwill,
you have stayed my friend
despite my surly bleats.
Humility, thou big liar, blest,
come out and take your part!

And get up, oh lecherous goat of a soul!
I want to be tripped on the leg
of the table of trouble,
toasted with the mopped-up wine
of playing a role.

Piñata

What a tangle we are,—
old whiskery God at his bowling alley
setting us up and knocking us about with questions
under the leaky roof of no-one can see.

And here comes that dirty old crone
like a witch, busy at her drudgery work
spinning and whacking the wheels and levers
of the work-a-day world.

So soon as we're born, we grasp what
we've been dropped into, and we try to clamber back.
But we must stay and share the absurdity
with its baffling pot-full of mysteries,

for the universe is mad, as all the poets alive and dead
have already seen, and it's time to whack the gay piñata
shaped like Batman in blue and green,
to stand in the shower raining down upon us

bonbons and sweets, while underneath
there's a fundament of deadly poison
bubbling and squeaking,
ready enough to keep us nimble on our feet.

Old Poet

Clouds don't come at him any more
seething inside with green fire, nor
does the skin of lovers often proclaim,
like a trumpet, fearful surprises.
And where are the river-roads that once he attended,
the quarrels that whistled around him like bullets,
the steaming tracks that swept him along come midnight
with the gift of a single mountain lantern?

Wherefrom are the words that used to hurt,
that hurt now twice as often,—
and where are the friends he loved enough to wish
he might give them a bit of his time on earth.
Also, old man, why can't left encounter right
anymore for a battle?
And where are the rattling snare drums of daylight?

Why do there not canter up these days
poems that stamp the hoof,
and offer the bridle, so he must clamber top-side
the saddle, and set himself to thunder off,
not caring to guess where the gallop goes,
or by what fork of the road,
or by what fork of the road.

AMBITION

Dante said ambition rose from hell.
Last week, beating upon my door,
it sat all smelly, in my waiting room,
sprawled devilish in my captain's chair.

Like a burlesque trooper, it yelled off-key
as I counted its weaknesses. It lied,
promised to clothe me with light,
like a holiday or a new year.

But I wondered what kind of a world it would be
if ambition were counted a sin,
and like a fiery torch came down far out on a lake,
with a fierce splash, and died away.

Or as sunrise, bushwhacked,
and only noticed
through the underbrush
as a yellow and murderous glow.

Orion on the Inside

Orion, you upstairs with your heavenly club and dog,
I leave you to your grand tangle,
but still dream of some grand epiphany to come.
Why do we bother to
waste a thought on those of us
who study the technique of learning
to be one of the arrogant pisspot leaders
who constantly arise and pay for our cheap blood.

The universe is a starry hive,
brother,
where we hunt from one conclusion to another,
only bigger, and most of us
have barely the wit to grasp
our hunger to be beside it.

Still, dogged brother halt a moment
to share with me what's to come,
what's been there for the taking
since there was a beginning,
and awaiting,
an adventure at the threshold of forever.

Fishermen

Out trolling the banks—the swirling rivers—the thump of the creel—
the fishermen seek a logical colloquy of wildlife and loaves
with shining words.
Then once in a while,
they watch their talismans over brutishness and power
go down, blighted by the savagery of fact.

As the civil world presses agreeably on
in its ramping, murderous way,
they come to be swept off like us all,
and forced to mouth the blameless blame.

Swearing to lies, they'll be wasted in the squalor,
but, after the cycles have inched about
another click,
with luck,
they'll cautiously hoist themselves
from out of the caves of hiding,
and once more casting to catch the shining words,
hang them like silver mornings in the sun.

WITCHES

I'd not lend them my ring,
but still anxious to hear what they'd say,
I came, uh! —through drizzle, cumulus and smoke
and gagged at their face,
cloaked and cowled about their pot.

I gave them the letter laying it out,
which they couldn't read.
They shredded it to dirt and sniffed.
I hated those nasty old girls behind their specs
leering and grinning! Idiots! At me cackling.

To flatter them, to pass the time,
I said that darkness liberates light.
That like the *Titanic*, it leans
on the verge of a black sea, shudders,
and drops out of sight—.

Lawk! They thought that was funny!
Laughed, snorted like a wolf's fart,
said, contemptuously,
"We are happiness, fool!

We're the dark old ladies without which
no dawn. We're the gold in the tomb,
the light woven in the burial cloth,
our glory the total emptiness of night!"

III

Goddam Pretty

When we were leaving that life,
we were so goddam pretty, so wildly young,—
two rumpled children, parked in a scratched
blue-light minibus just in time for collapsing dusk—
amid popcorn and coffee,
ransacking our kids' diapers under the murky dome light.

You were brown in corduroy, shimmery with blond locks,
climbing to the wheel and weaving the car,
thoughtlessly pelting in and out among the beetling trucks.
The memory pleads remember me
though now the car is locked so tight,
its door ground shut with a set brace,
that I'm not allowed even a thank-you, anymore.
That's a given.

To look twice in that uncurtained window
would be too much—
something like death, and I will not,
if it is going to smatter of goodbyes,
or anything like that, well, no, damn it!

Yet the fiercely demanding memory
shifts the years once more however they grind and scrape,
to wherever you are,
and once again you are calming the kids as only you know how,
shaking out your shimmering hair,
taking the driver's seat,
and turning the wheel faithlessly,
moving us away like long ago messengers to the North.

Issa

Issa, who lost two wives and three babes
in the service of the simple,
Socrates, Lord of the Cup,
Mayakovsky, riding his trigger,
Villon his appetite and fleas—
bless them, those who offered
a single life climbing the ramparts,
who willingly fell like break-through fighters
stricken upon the weapons of the damned.

Sing, as we set out to overturn the world
even if the Gods judge us
not worth the flex to kick around,
do not let it trouble you,
be born to do what's right—
whatever the day or week.
Unhinge them, distract them,
and guide them right and wrong with a holy song.

Bears

"Pooh, when I grow up, will you remember me?"
— CHRISTOPHER ROBIN

It was the Hotel de Calais,
    around the corner from
the Place De La Concorde,
    and I was six.

One morning, word
    gusted away down the corridors
like a smoke or a vapor,
    "Les Milnes sont arrivees!"

I longed to see that most famous
    little boy in the world
stuffed with an armload
    of bear and pig,

flown here out of
    the Hundred Acre Wood.
All I had was a cardboard pencil case
    they gave me when I bought new shoes.

I hung it out the window
    held up I thought by a blue gas balloon,
but while I slept the night
    the gas went away

and left the pencil case and balloon
        to fall from the window
down
        into the street below.

There was a gendarme on the corner
        who pointed his finger at me. I cried.
Clearly the world
        cared nothing at all

for what or who I was.
        I decided,
shutting the hinge on time,
        that I would never grow up,

and so, I never have,
        whatever the disguise.
The world is such a hateful place to be
        and never safe,

filled with killing and lying, I swore
        I'd shut my wits up
and
        find my own way home.

And so I did, and so I always do,
        and to this day I'm just the right size.
And still, says Pooh,
        he'll forever remember me.

The View from Straw's

Here, two fluttering counties are taking a wink,
up amphitheaters, right and left,
bending over hillocks into empty air,
rope-walking birds skim past beneath.

The woods run down below,
across creek lines,
slithering like snakes, hobo blankets
molting onto brown remembrances,
against the powers of hayfield and wood.
The gypsy moth has crept with needlesome jaw
across the green world fading like a scrim.

Murder hides behind our little tract,
he's a bony devil, knuckle lumps
rapping his frying pan, while underneath,
the crack of terror burns.

Up country the furious beasts of pandemonium
wildly devour each others tails,
and seesaws rise and fall across Galactic gulfs,
a bucket of water rises in the Malacca Strait,
upping the level in Chile, and spattering on our shore.

But for the moment, our premiums paid,
we hang transfixed up the tattered air
where merely to sleep and wake is to walk through miracles.
Higher than eagles, here comes luck,
making a bargain with the hungry firmament.

THE BANDERLOG*

At the nursing home, mischievous spidery creatures,
adversely, they're creeping down on the gates of hell,
hand clasped in hand, glittering like tortoiseshell.
Their murmur of gods is only to lull the young—.
Fierce of dreams, they are full of scorn—
who want it no more, though stamped with its parts,
and therefore they gamble,—betting against their hearts.

Watch their shadows dance as lonely as bones in Plato's cave!
They throw back ragged kisses to what they were,
and wildly miss—by galaxies— lost times misremembered,
half-hopes misplaced. — What do you need, — we ask.
They snicker. We own the gift no more than a star or a fly.
Still, they wink us well with one remaining
crooked, yellow, humorous eye.

*Kipling's monkeys

Seamstress of Shine

Not knowing whereupon to rattle,
I hereupon struggle to find my drum.
Taking in my hands
the skirts of the real,
I stitch them with twine.

Soon enough, secretly
the art of stealing comes arise,
rushing through my wrists,
in out, in out it flies.
And out of that handicraft, such élan!
Old profligate, making a gift of himself
to the mistress of bees, the seamstress of shine!

Parlay and Whine

This varisome globe that swirls
on gimbal pins of prayers,
begets a sort of musical ache
not ministered to by the mumbles of the spheres.

With livid whorl and puffing lip
from the wild tuba-storm,
it grumbles and sings on summer afternoons,
endlessly calling the roll of the vows,
proclaiming the parturition
of a new world from blood and rain.

But is it truly more than a moment
of angel wing and rainbow shine,
passing along the ever loquacious
paternosters of parlay and whine?

Sunset Rock

"Said Billy Rose to Sally Rand"

Father Sun is just settled down in a red haze
up the farthest slope of the Ramapos, when suddenly out
from the dusk with a rushing and a tinkling,
we're assailed by spectral shadows. They swirl our way
down through the sun-careening fire-dazzled woods.

They're the show girls, draped in Jean Harlow dresses
scissored down to the buttock-nape.
They shriek tinnily in high double heels, giggling and slipping
on shiny Philippine grass, they spill their bathtub gin
and stand for a moment, lifting their glasses
to toast the sun's wild footlights off to the West.

They've tittered like ghosts down from Billy Rose's house
on the rise behind, with its English windows and gray slate roof,
its paneled jazz-age rooms.
By the old liquor closet at the unused central flue,
you can almost hear the Volstead dicks come ghosting up the drive,
with a wail, from Wampus Pond and Armonk, down below.

They've come, with a great scattering and screeching and to-do,
draining the bathtubs, the ghostly vermouth and juniper juice,
pouring it out among the actual roots
of the memory trees, where they soar
skyward, like the joyous dream of a lark.

None of them glows in the effulgent sunset
or lays out what blazing road goes by, opens a ghostly door
or fades the light down silent driveways of the imagination.
They are frolicking, a thing and a place where we can never be or go.
Salute their voyage!

Us

The vicious world keeps banging at our door,
while that morning splendor in the east
explodes in orange, amethyst, and solferino,
and the tragic barque of the world once more hoves to,
deck after deck loaded with autos fit to skid,
hookers and dealers making book in the customary way.

Lying us, who live off the honesty of animals!
We train ourselves to believe
asylum awaits us in the skies.
How rescue the dreamers of the future, of tomorrow,
away from these pitiful ceremonies of hell?

There's little choice. We're famously stubborn,
must live this way,
and like any other day, beg for more, suppliant,
in a world which treats us like a near-dead child,
lost and abandoned beside our own door.

Skyline

"Mais ou sont les neiges d'antan?/"
> — Francois Villon

In memory of Fletcher and Inga Pratt

The skyline is foretelling, with its usual mystic fistula,
what's to come,
as we ring the Pratt's bell, and climb the stairs
to that lavish disheveled, vast frigate
forever casting off and around Columbus Circle
to dock at Central Park.

The tumbled decks thrive with Dictaphones,
marmosets, models of battleships, blinking girls,
life disguising itself with gossamer, lying, and illusions of ecstasy.
It's only a ramshackle dream, but he's paid
a weary admission to things that sneer and grasp and slam
that hurt awfully because they're gone.
Back come back, he beseeches the shimmering past!

Once for an hour or two, he'd such companions—
David Garrick spying through the keyhole
on Doctor Johnson's honeymoon with Tetty,
Sheridan eloping with Lizzy Lindsey out of the house
where Emma Hamilton shucked the beds as upstairs maid,
where Evelyn got his oranges off Nell Gwynne,
and Peter the Great is renting a garden, learning to sail
down the Thames flats, waving at Pepys and his brass spyglass.

Here we read all day long
the entries in each other's eyes,
rustling the springs of a hundred trunks,
uncle, toad, bawd of the Prince of Wales,
toy, wink, devil and bad mistake.
Our illusions are practicing how to live,
and somehow happiest now
misted in the shifting clouds of a scribbler's dream.

But infant and quonmdam prince, he must learn to be thankful
for any opening door,
content with making do, grasping for an instant the precious
        chalice
that shines and vanishes. A risk the proud man
stays forever shackled to.

Dante explained it was like fire.
You crouch with impossibilities, the ugly and hateful,
the earnest, the humorless, the bilious, forever,
until that day you enter upon the dreadful dark,
around the knees of some vile maggoty mountain
and surprise! Enter on what you've become,
a sort of dancing floor, beneath the riot of stars.

The Spell Coming On

To Bobby

When the spell came on
he'd gather about him four or five accustomed to this journey,
content to sit spellbound
a couple hour or two in thrall,
and he'd begin to speak,
like warming an instrument.

The subject, what came to him this particular moment, —
a divertissement
about Japanese bathhouse customs, the history of weather,
how to construct a university out of sticks and stones,
being a biochemical race-mixer
in the bellybutton of the South.

It was always a trip like dashing and wandering
through hill country on a company bus,
whanging and sheeting water between vegetable rows,
flying, snapping tree branches,
with bundles of interruptions dropping like events
in the middle of happening,
or parcels of accidental newspapers,
from posterity delivered along imaginary routes.

With a stop for breath, he'd plunge on
through towns and slums across the lanes
where sunlight and shadow snapped and blared,
and eventful fact and fruitful wish

crashed on top of one another like waves
or ragweed and kale tumbled in the harvest.

Someone incredulous, hearing for the first time
this obbligato of words and pictures,
accused him of being a poet.

Laughing, eyes somber, –Bobby shook his head.
"You mistake the nature of poetry.
I'm more a traveling agriculturalist,
setting out plants as I go.

Hoping a few will be lucky enough to root and catch.
Above the whoosh of the tires and the whisk of the water
—sometime with luck, I hope, through the highway clatter,
because I'm filled with delight,
it will make a kind of music.
I'm only witness to the song."

IV

A Visit to Barbados

Not our singing sort of bird, instead, they scream,
harpies screeching across the reef.
The shallow harbor foams a motley green,
and rising from its snaky arbor,
a tunic of dark wood crawls up the island breast
escaping into tropical dreams,
building from driftwood,
its palaces of kingdom come.

Above, a lowering purple mountain rides,—
Goddess of desire, pressing a lazy haunch
against the luxuriant sky. A puttering launch,
a pilot yawning, thumps the indifferent tide.
Where pirates anchored, throngs of beach boys ride.

Today we lunch at the inn
upon a verandah spread three sides,
then spend afternoon climbing the spur of a hill
to watch how the sunset drops with a thump
and night falls down like a violent thief.

Then the dark is stung with a hive
of hissing kerosene lamps
and amid them we seek our temporary home
down from the jungle on rented double wheels,
down the rutted road slowly feeling the way,
till we come to the clear asphalt
and let the pedals fly.

Of a sudden, children playing by the road
begin to follow where we go,
a running, screaming Creole crowd,
to see two grown-up elderly kids
go flying past in the dark. They ran, we fled,
in the name of terror.

They tried to catch us in the name of fun
till we came to the edge of what they called "the town"
and they suddenly stopped like a song-less choir
blown up out of blackness,
lighting its watchful but indifferent train of fire.

Glittering

I'm bound with this brother,
this animal, this glittering word like a beast,
in pairs, with wire,
for I distrust him, he mistrusts me, too.
That hungry wastrel is not sure
if he'd prefer to live on dirt or fire,
and howls like a dog to keep me from my sleep.
Finding in this no splendor,—in his puzzlement, he curses
whatever rag or plume my reticence wears this week.

He grinds his spectral teeth at the claims of linen and love,
dotes on dramatic hates and sleek defeats,
and will be the master soon enough (he thinks).
He'll catch me bending,
start me off upon my daily wreck,
make me howl, run mad, for all my shape and reason.
Size and weight to him are prose,
Time's vicious fabulist that baits me by the nose.

Chocolate Pie

Fred's great chocolate pie
sat on the table at noon—
while outside the spring sun dazzled, leapt,
and the Germans marched into Austria.

On the radio came shouts, in a hoarse, hysterical voice,
the future jangled their wits like a telephone.
Our appointed war was waiting for us outside, cocking its thumb.

"Arma virumque cano," says Virgil.
Dr. Cutt snakes out the words with a dry, ironic, bite,
saying, "This is the war
your generation is set up to perish for,
because my own was an idiot,
and savors itself with the gruel of madness.
The legend says
if you must plant hatred, stay on guard
and lop the heads off the warriors
springing from the ground.
Do it again and again!
But this time, for a change, stay home."

It was certainly not for lack of battlegrounds.
We've plenty of those at hand.
Not ten miles away, at Stones River,
Generals Rosecrans and Bragg
waltzed one another a half turn
about the Murfreesboro Pike.
You can picnic among the twenty-five thousand dead.

At Spring Hill, Patrick Cleburne, "bravest of the brave,"
let Schofield's Yankees slip through.
And the next day, under the scattershot of John Hood's rage,
he charged himself to death with five other rebel generals.
They lay in a row on the Carnton House porch,
fury assuaged.

Down the Nashville Pike came
General Thomas racketing through,
flogging his horse,
yelling across the clatter
'Didn't we drive 'em though? Didn't we drive 'em!"
And Forrest's horse lagged to guard the retreat.

Grandpa lived in the saddle for days
near the surgeon's wagon taking out his surgical kit
to patch the few come out alive,
subsiding into Alabama.

That, was our war.
What did we know about motorized guns on wheels,
or hawks-foot bombers diving out of the sun?

Circe

Odyssey—book 10

Lost in the mouth of luck,
we felt many times lost
in the overmastering seas,
but came at length,
straddling the backbone of timber,
through five days of wild lightning

booming up to an island
not accounted for in the weather,
where being without help,
we were turned into swine.

Oh Gods! Where is our following wind?
Or any Goddess coming to be of help?
We had escaped old monster One-eye.
(Damn his flax in the locks)
he'd slipped up on us treading like velvet.

But now comes this.
The she-thing we have feared the most.
Because it is literate and temperate,
and devours us with truth and argument.
When she talks we dare not breathe.
She sniffs like a harrier.

We've made ourselves ready to pay her price
for that fearful thing She calls love.

At last, we've given up, even in thought,
but we are human and being human,
live on dreams.
We've arrived at being more like a pig than a pig.
Appetite swallows us.

Rudderless

> *With back to the sea, you must wander till you*
> *meet those in the road who mistake your oars for*
> *winnowing fans.*
>
> — Homer

My car is parked someplace I cannot claim to be,
in a venomous world where poor lost souls,
Inferno bound, dreary the passage
chained in the trappings of half-lived lives.

How evade this world of pain but through stealth?
As Homer said, fire is rudderless,
and you will most likely be scorched
in combat with the world.

Yet one thing stubbornly labors to fly,
and not be whipped like a dog off a cliff,
while it struggles with Jesus
against the spinning of money.

We must come in the end
to put our faith in those
who've rescued themselves from hate
before us. Vast innocent souls

like Van Gogh and Thoreau,—
Issa, Mozart, Basho, Einstein,
(trimming his sailing boat of space,
gliding down the zipper of science, whistling).

People who couldn't live
however they tried, any place but right.
So up they rose, shortening as they flew,
alive in the Greece of the poets,

rocked in the arms of tendrilly father octopus,
mindful of the seas singing and groaning,
but awake and learning to tell an oar
from a winnowing fan.

Fly Ball

Grandpa shagging flies
In the Civil War dusk
Once the horses were picketed
If nobody turned up sick or shot.

Daddy wound twine about cork,
Sewed horsehide to make a ball, a century past,
Helping him stitch in surgery
Or stretching for wild throws
Under the town crag by the Elk Creek.

The stiff lacing
Cuffed the fingers so
What's the delicious remnant,
The swivel of whack!
Aha! Or slipping it past them.

Some Baltimore chop
A downward blow
That escapes itself sunward,
Up bounding beyond reach
Plashing the creeks of rough and private sky.

Weaving

Devious Cain sang his way to the scaffold,
and laughed, (sneak thief of breath),
that he'd put one over on us,
while the sun and the moon sprung the trap.
We thought we'd seen him kicking and hanged,
but God, nearby, only shook his head,
and stayed busy picking scrap.

Stringing sweet pith to fear,
we knitted a hangman's rope,
and out of our bale-fire rage,
we wove from nothing sufficient guilt
to make our lot seem worth its salt.

So now we've learnt to wear with pride,
that fake blazing diadem, and having got that far,
put our thumb under God's thumb,
and hoarding knots against the grain,
weave the night against the braid of day.

PUTTING TOGETHER MORNING

It's putting together Morning
out of broken shards and fractured rifts, —
as with crippled feet —
what's twisted, yaws,
and hankers after straight,
and while up East, light fumbles its way
through the bowels of dark
like a lost messenger, and
keeps hallooing after mistakes,
from nowhere comes a spatter-dash of rain
rumbling down the canyons from above.

Suddenly, out of the zenith,
the hinges of light turn, like enormous rocks,
and with no effort and no sound,
bound for the azimuth,
upward plunges the sun.

Crannies of the Mind

*"Rival ideologies almost always are a way of
sanctifying the aims of the cunning in the eyes of
the foolish and the dull."*
— Marguerite Yourcenar

The Fifth World War was fought on schedule by the book
and as across the marketplace the horrors skipped,
grenades sputtered in the safe houses of the mind.
Confusion drifted amongst the battlements
forcing thieves and customers alike to burrow
deep for their share of the blame.

When the front broke, the enemy put on the face
of innocent neighbors coming to call.
And since the enemy was hiding in our heart
God felt he should humor our compulsion to love
in the name of hate,
and since in his name we fought
and cornered the most outrageous words,
he locked them up in the bank.

Thus our wits kept running amok,
in the stolen crannies of the mind,
preparing to attack the dangerous parts of speech,
while the aristocracy of the brain
we always trusted, has long since finished its laugh,
and gone to sleep like a drunk
who snores in a crook of the stairs.

If Suffering Is to Love

An addled warrior like the rest of us,
your heart is a spear without aim
that fells both enemy and friend.
When the red witch invites,
you storm the gate
savoring the pothole in every wonder.

For if you must be safe and live in bricks,—
make straw from dryness,
hop low and bend not,
with all that balance and teetering,
do you think you'll say goodbye to risk?

What lives is the prisoner of luck.
We water the gift of thinking blessedly good
what cannot help but be so.
Don't fly ahead of or behind the sun.
Be alive, fear circumstance and shut one eye.

If suffering is to love
that's what was intended.
It's whence we came
and what we spend a lifetime
learning to be about.

TREES

In memory of Adele de la Barre Robinson

It was a strange wood in which she decided
to consider herself lost.
It was filled with sun at cool angles,
Sylvanum densiflora, bracken,
live trees with lulling voices.
Trunks of bodies starting from the earth like plants.
Screams without throats,
Lianas tangled in unnamable wildness—
a world which would not accept order.

Existence snuffled with warty nozzle about this stranger
unacquainted with mere fact,
but who did not evade its vilest bubblings and quakings.
She would not draw back from the black crevasses,
which allowed her to name it a name,
imagine it to a shape it had not become
except as a neighbor to fear.
She recollected a prophet who spoke from a tree.

At first doubtfully, then gratefully, at last
brimming with courage, became what
was determined to take her,
and turning it inside out,
grew herself into death and gave it her soul.

V

Tomorrow I'll Be Gone

I'll go west up the cart path
first thing this morning
to the top of the Palisades,
and coming around the edges of old rock quarries
       spring
       once,
in a certain way—
and sail out over the river
      like an angel.
From up there
at last I will take a long look
     at the sunrise,
     with nothing whatever in the way.
Not a worry or consideration
     about refueling,
no vibration sickness,
not a reminder of the time for coffee.
I will slide out over Block Island
     and Sandy Hook.
Maybe I will flap off to Europe,
     maybe not.
Who knows how I will feel under those circumstances?
     Anyway,
I will be back for dinner
upon the chimneys of the White House
     served upon confusion of purpose
and loftiness of aim.
I will be given a free ticket
     upon the Pennsylvania Railroad,

     but I will not be troubled to use it.
Of course it will not be long
before the whole world
will have set out to look for me
obsessed with what it will call patriotism
     or commitment or admiration,
by which it will mean inverted love.
And while I am dropping strawberries with notes from above,
everybody will be plodding
     around through the snow
     in astrakhans and knee boots
asking for me.
But in every case, as they arrive,
I will have just that minute come in
     through the front door
and taken wing at the back.

Shipwrecked upon a Seacoast in Bohemia

— Hooper and Donna

He spoke orations like a stream full of bumping logs,
sported legal erudition like a Blackstone larynx,
brave head wrapped like a turban in precedential fog.

Called Hooper, he was a tall, luminous paragon of the law
whose humor hovered over a quiver-full of jokes.
like a lion advancing a congratulatory paw.

He cheerfully scattered about himself as though from the roof
vast pronouncements like three-winged eagles,
absentmindedly shot them down with a hyperextended spoof.

Till the day came he met Donna, whose exciting battle of words
had been played out up north
in the home of the Broadway Theatre Birds.

Now she came flopping home like kingdom come
to settle for what was at hand
with ample illusion left to strike us dumb.

Unfailingly she was, as ever, theatrical, airy,
playing life off the tips of disdainful fingers.
Squirt, squirt, distributing the goodies, like a perspicacious fairy,

dropping one over there, two over here, ploop! ploop!
"So be it! If you don't like it, dearie,
send an Email to my chicken soup!"

She was constructed like the bay bridge, all distances and loops,
in the clothes she made herself freehand, shaping the cloth
in romantic, visionary, scissor swoops.

Her full-length opera cloak,
included the hunt, the hunters, a dozen dogs, the deer,
and coming from behind, athwart the smoke,

a trumpeter signaling their approach
by honking the hours to his horse
and welcoming them to an inn with an approaching coach.

She'd happily turn and show you the panorama.
As she perceived it, life was the fluttery
festive commedia of a swiftly revolving diorama.

Their meeting—(it did come)—was as though Blackbeard the Pirate,
pistoleros smoking, climbed aboard
some gold-laden galleon with his shrieking parrot.

Such explosions! They huffed, joked, laughed, circled, sang,
challenged one the other, like craziness,
each clanging the other as though the Liberty Bell had rung.

Who was the audience, who were the performers?
At length, spent, like blown-out Etnas and Krakatoas,
they fell asleep in separate terra firmas.

If Bonaparte had entered the room with Pitt the Younger, no doubt
they'd have quickly learned the rule. One or both must depart.
Two grand styles cancel each other out.

Overheard in a Drugstore

It's as I said, and you know I'd never lie! —
I've got to believe in God.
He's not the fashion, that's what makes him mine!
I mean the intelligent God we're fond of talking about,
who almost summons up the wit to solve a problem.
Think of all the time the Universe took,
managing those infinite batches of particles,
and how much it took to fashion one galaxy,
never mind those tiresome billions,
moving them all in the right direction,
about the inflating universe. And also, I've heard
scientists say,—who ought to know,—
that he's stowed what they call "dark matter"
away in some closet full of the cosmos, until he's got time
to make a smidgen of something interesting or useful about it.

But to get back where I was, I can't endure for anything,
or any person, to get ahead of me. "It's a quirk of my personality,"
says my dad,—who has the same peculiar failing.
If, back in school, the other children brought
their wax panpipes to class, I spat out my own and
bought a hatchet.

Dad's a lot like me. —I remember he sat in a tree once,
for three weeks, back there at the end of the Depression,
but came down in disgust on hearing
he'd engineered a fad. He couldn't bear
to be just one of two, and I'm as much like him
as he could stand.

But I digress. I've got to have my God unpopular,
which brings up item one—to wit—*i.e.*
I think we come here many times!
I will not have a God who's such a miser,
(think of all that dark matter),
a greedy grub so measuring grams in spoons,
that he'd revolve us once this way for life,
then farm us out on universal pensions.
Preserve me from such a wretched, hanky-panky God,
who has all the earnest conscience of a slave,
—no offense intended!

        My mother says
I reason like a Prussian. Great old dame,
she knows more than she ought to know!
Truth is, they botched me at my last transubstantiation.
They cast us like hot bronze, you know, almost like
old statues in new molds—which is—with the smoke
and the swearing, quite a lot like
Benevento Cellini cursing and rummaging
through the junk of Florence,
looking for odds and ends of bronze
to finish the "Perseus."

        They'd got my new mold ready for the flux—
and had melted my old substance in the fire,
but a whistle blew somewhere for a change of shift,
and they lost their heads, so, wreathed in smoke, they poured
the not quite melted stuff, and choked the spout.
So I'm a reject.

        That's why my left leg is shorter than the right—see?—so help me.

(Willy Nilly here, I was a Prussian once).
There are two men mixed up in me like nuts in fudge!
The Prussian part was sabered at Sedan.
He spends his life complaining how he died.
Because, I think, that newly tempered part,
closest to his center, melted last.
It's from him I learned about cuirasses.
I'm sure I've never seen one. (—Body armor,
obsolete after 1453, but kept because it flattered the cavalry.)
We called it "going to chase the fire in the stove,
with the scuttle for a headpiece."

    So I was at Sedan;
my horse sweating, saber in my hand,
ahead a cloud of smoke and a tatter of blue sky.
There's always another crooked to be made straight,
and this is like that,—also—,
like an escape from a castle prison in a Dumas novel,
always an opening door, (the breath in the throat),
disclosing another door and lock ahead, full of questions.

    —But I gravely under-dramatize the thing—
this is all that, yes, all that—but with the further twist,
the fierce uncertainty, of being unprepared!
Of having to go out with a smile to meet,
while never knowing what, at God's pounce,
you're supposed to need to know, or do, or say!

    You think I'm here for a prescription,
which is true enough, but also
I'm waiting for the time when, as I'll explain in a moment,
I find myself dead.

OVERHEARD IN A DRUGSTORE / 79

Obviously of course—God knows—
I've not been called on quite as yet!
It may be years or weeks,—or, goodness, help me—
any moment! One might banter jokes
with a lewd disease, murder a child for its peppermint,
putty a window, eat a roll. Impossible to say!
You think I'm talking nonsense, but it's sense to God!
He hasn't any morals, or, in a way, the least sense of proportion.

      I know a few things. One of them is that
this Prussian in me came from the time before.
And because of him, I'm still afraid of horses,
like a smashed race driver that's afraid of cars.
I shudder, passing a stable, I hate the things.
But I've a notion what I'm fated for, next time.
I'm to be called up—boot and spur—to ride
like Genghis Khan strapped on some damn pony,
to Samarkand. I rather fancy
that's what God would have to have of me. A test!
That wicked sense of humor of his, will make my life be horses,
knowing I'd rather be blind than look in a horse's eye.

GROUCHO

I'm the Groucho of friendship, which means
nobody I'd like for a friend
could stand to be friends with me.
But never mind, I'm an actor,
I play them all, the stinking policemen,
the rude nursemaids, the dumb blondes at the ball.
I'm a history of comedy delineated by whine.

That creature we call our director
controls the debacle I call the passage of time.
On good days my secret hope
is that I can spend him on what he thinks is me,
then hang myself by a counterfeit note.

Each day I shovel dirt at the top of the heap,
run below to see what revelation
tumbles out of the mill
then cheer me up by checking
what puzzlement I represent.

For my secret name is Dollar Bill, and I
wait for the bank to open at some o'clock,
whoever I am that minute can hardly wait
to turn the key, open the register,
and pop me in the till!

Lobotomy

I said it's true my reach exceeds my grasp,
but I've hauled my soul up out of the reach of the sea.

When they sent an ambulance to claim my remains
four white angels, set with calloused knobs, staked a claim on me.

They wrestled me for what was left.
I strove all day and woke up in a week
bereft of part of my brain.

At least I never dream.
All my desires are written on a critique at the foot of my bed,
foolscap kept conveniently by my feet.

I write down when they tell me smile or nod
for happy at last, losing it was a gas!
Is what remains godliness or merely sassafras?

It gives me joy these days
that whatever anyone wishes to say
on any subject, I happily agree!

What's left, is more than enough;
I applaud everything with what's left of me.

If a Body

A Cadaverous Lament

> *in the footsteps of . . . Bobby Burns*
> *caught comin' through the rye*

If cadaver meet cadaver
walkin' down the street,

they exchange cadaverous greetin's
where cadavers meet.

Every body's got a body
plastered sheet to sheet,

an' every gurney ends its journey
where the bedpans meet!

If cadaver meet cadaver
comin' from the toon,

they exchange cadaverous grinnings
ne'er a ghastly froon.

Everybody's got a body
none they swear hae yee,

yet all the slops come lick their chops
as they lay doon and dee.

Repartee

A pied old codger tossed his drooling chin
captiously as he crossed and intertwined his eyes.
"Youngster," he wailed (he sucked his whiskers in),
"because of them great disturbances in the skies

there where the aircraft fizz, or yonder where the groves
is all spring blossoms, calibrating blood and bones and skin,
and something gallops off burning the pitiful loaves
and spoiling the fishes, I've settled up with men.

The thing God emphasized to me this afternoon
bears taking thought. (He lives like me, in a cave—
not giving a kopeck for this wilderness of hate)."
At which the old coot wove a nod to some phantasm up from its grave.

A sort of pain crossed his wrinkles (wild and funny,
as only suffering can be). "God and me, come to an agreement.
Our best bet—give up the world, go happy insane,
just HIM, and you, and me!"

The Life of a Gnat

"Christy's Song" from The Most Engaged Girl,
music by Alan Hovhaness, book and lyrics by Andrew Glaze

The life of a gnat is so simple and straight
as she crawls in the palm of your hand.
She's born in the dawn, at the heart of the dew,
and she dries out her wings in the sun.
Then she flies with her love,
tiny, tiny love,
with her love, only hers,
tiny love but true.

The moon rolls around through the sky in the night
all alone in the wind and the dark.
She knows where she goes she has only got one,
and revolves in the light of her love.
Once a year in his arms,
reeling round the sky
with her love, only hers,
clasped in the arms of her sun.

The life of a girl is nothing like that,
though I wish and I dream that it were.
I look for the one that will set me afire
or dance me all day in the wind.
I would swim through the sky
if I thought he were there,
I would fly through the air
to capture my lonely desire.

You're Never with Who You Want to Be

You're never with who you want to be
so stand up and take your pill.
While Jill Hathaway was making hay,
her sister was making Will.

And Josephine loved a financier
while Bonaparte loved a Pole.
You're never with who you want to be
you've got to play a role.

When Plato came home to Mrs. Plato
she smiled at him so coy.
She might have saved herself the trouble
he much preferred a boy.

While Romeo waited for Juliet
she's engaged to another man.
You're never with who you want to be,
it's part of nature's plan.

When Antony died, he called for Cleo
while making his dying gasp,
but she's up in a tower taking her ease
and lying down with an asp.

While Caesar was up in Gaul with his troop,
dividing it with his life,
three men in Rome were drawing straws
dividing up Caesar's wife.

The time will come when you've left your Frankie
and run off with Nellie Bly, but while you're embracing,
her eye will light
on someone passing by.

So as you lead the parade of life
the band plays just one tune.
You're going to be with the one you want
when Christmas comes in June.